Plate I.

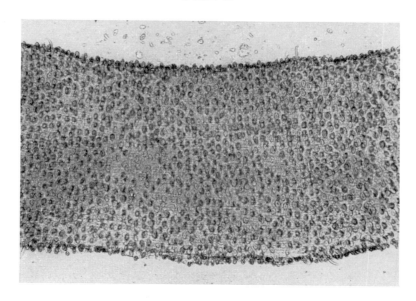

A. Surface view of the body-wall of *Peloscolex ferox* to show papillae.

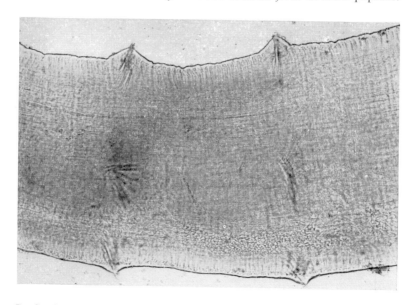

B. Surface view of *Limnodrilus hoffmeisteri* to show the usual condition, without papillae.

A GUIDE FOR THE IDENTIFICATION OF

BRITISH

Aquatic Oligochaeta

by

R. O. BRINKHURST, Ph.D.

University of Toronto

FRESHWATER BIOLOGICAL ASSOCIATION

SCIENTIFIC PUBLICATION No. 22

Second Edition, revised, 1971

FOREWORD

For many years the oligochaete worms have been a stumbling block in faunistic survey work in fresh water. This has been all the more regrettable because of the part the Tubificidae have long been recognized as playing in the fauna where streams and rivers are affected by organic pollution. Freshwater ecologists will therefore have cause to be grateful to Dr Brinkhurst for the work he has done on the group during the last few years, and for the keys which have resulted in this publication.

In the present imperfect state of our knowledge it has not seemed possible to compile distribution maps that would do more than show the distribution of collectors and their activities, but we hope that an easy means of identification will lead to a flow of records, which will be warmly welcomed either here at The Ferry House or by Dr Brinkhurst himself. In a future edition we shall hope to include maps.

THE FERRY HOUSE,
May 1963.

H. C. GILSON,
Director.

SBN 900386 15 0

CONTENTS

INTRODUCTION

This group of animals has the reputation of being very difficult to identify, largely because of the absence of taxonomic revisions and the need for careful microscopic study of mounted material. In the last few years the position has improved with the publication of systematic reviews of the Naididae (Sperber 1948, 1950), Enchytraeidae (Nielsen & Christensen 1959), and Tubificidae (Brinkhurst 1963a), and now an account of the world aquatic Oligochaeta has been prepared (Brinkhurst & Jamieson — 1971).

Keys to the Aeolosomatidae, Naididae, Lumbriculidae, Dorydrilidae and Tubificidae include all known British species (Brinkhurst 1966), but in the other families the procedure is a little different. The key to families will direct the reader to sections dealing with the Enchytraeidae, Haplotaxidae, Glossoscolecidae, Lumbricidae and Branchiobdellidae. No attempt has been made to compile keys to the Enchytraeidae as most species are not aquatic. Instead the reader is directed to the recent taxonomic study by Nielsen & Christensen (1959) in which keys to genera and descriptions of European species will be found. As there is only a single aquatic species in each of the remaining families, a brief description of the animal concerned is given in each instance. As several Lumbricidae (true earthworms) are occasionally found in aquatic environments, reference is made to the most recent key, after the description of the single species usually encountered in freshwater. The Branchiobdellidae are included although I have no certain British record, but no keys to species are given. It is hoped, then, that with this publication it will be possible to identify to species all truly aquatic Oligochaeta that have been recorded from Britain, with the exception of those few Enchytraeidae which can be said to be truly aquatic. In addition, references to Brinkhurst & Jamieson should make it possible to name species not yet recorded from Britain if these remain to be discovered, as seems highly probable.

Although it is to be hoped that this publication will make it easier than before to identify aquatic Oligochaeta, it should be noted that it is necessary to make a microscopical preparation (albeit by a very simple method) of each individual, and that it may be necessary to use an oil immersion lens to study the fine details of chaetal form. In some instances mature specimens will be required for certain identification, but on the whole the chaetae are the principal features employed in these keys. The genera of the Tubificidae are defined chiefly by the form of the male efferent ducts (fig. 7), but as these are not always readily visible in whole mounts, reference to these structures is omitted from the key, which proceeds straight to species. Those wishing additional confirmation of identification can dissect mature specimens (even after they have been cleared by the technique described below) to obtain the ducts.

PREPARATION OF MATERIAL

AEOLOSOMATIDAE, NAIDIDAE, TUBIFICIDAE, HAPLOTAXIDAE, LUMBRICULIDAE, DORYDRILIDAE

The worms may be killed and preserved in 70% alcohol, with the exception of *Branchiura sowerbyi* which tends to fragment. Luckily this is the one oligochaete which is immediately recognisable in the field. This must be narcotised in 5% magnesium chloride before preservation.

Preserved worms may be stored in 70% alcohol. When required for identification, they should be transferred to 30% alcohol and then to water. They are next placed on a slide in a few drops of Amman's lactophenol, prepared as follows:

Carbolic acid	400 g
Lactic acid	400 ml
Glycerol	800 ml
Water	400 ml

The worms should be covered with a coverslip and left in this fluid for several hours before examination. The time will depend on the size and maturity of the specimen. Just before examining, slight pressure on the coverslip will flatten the specimen and render the important features more readily visible.

If a permanent preparation be required, the Amman's lactophenol can be replaced by polyvinyl lactophenol. When this has dried sufficiently the preparation should be ringed, preferably in 'Glyceel'.

GLOSSOSCOLECIDAE, ENCHYTRAEIDAE, LUMBRICIDAE

These worms are mostly too large to be prepared in the above fashion. The Enchytraeidae are suitable in size but as the chaetae are mostly similar in form within a genus, experts in the taxonomy of this group prefer to examine material alive. Whole mounts prepared in the above fashion may be identified to genera, but usually not to species.

Mature specimens of the Glossoscolecidae and Lumbricidae may be identified using only a low-power stereoscopic microscope.

EXAMINATION OF WHOLE MOUNTS

The first point to remember about the anatomy of the oligochaetes is that the first segment is devoid of chaetae* (fig. 1) which are otherwise arranged in four bundles on each segment, two dorso-lateral (termed dorsal) bundles and two ventro-lateral (termed ventral) bundles.† In many Naididae the dorsal bundles begin on a more posterior segment in fully developed specimens. It should, however, be stressed that when asexual reproduction occurs, daughter individuals are budded off, and these frequently develop the most anterior segments last of all, so that some specimens may appear to have the dorsal chaetae starting in segment II when they are quoted in the key as being more posterior. With practice these worms can be recognised as detached asexually-produced forms, from the absence of the prostomium, and in any case the parent specimen is usually present in the collection.

The principle features to study are the chaetae. These may be of several types. In determining the various sorts of chaetae in a specimen, dorsal and ventral chaetal bundles from several regions of the body should be examined.

Hair chaetae are more or less elongate slender filaments, present in all bundles in the Aeolosomatidae and only in the dorsal bundles of

---

* Most authors use the term setae in preference to chaetae.
† The standard work in English on the morphology of the Oligochaeta is Stephenson (1930). See also Brinkhurst & Jamieson (1971).

many Naididae and Tubificidae. They sometimes bear fine lateral hairs which are employed in the key to the Naididae but ignored in the Tubificidae where they are difficult to see. They are unusually broad in the tubificid genus *Peloscolex*.

Bifid crotchets are found in both dorsal and ventral bundles in the Naididae, Tubificidae and Lumbriculidae. They are S-shaped structures with the distal end bifurcate, and it is the form of these

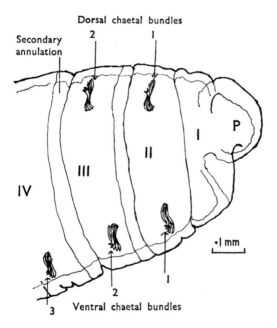

Fig. 1. The anterior end of an oligochaete worm (*Limnodrilus hoffmeisteri*) to show the relationship between the segments and the chaetal bundles. Note that chaetae are absent from segment 1.

teeth and their relative length which is commonly referred to in the key. The distal ends of some bifid crotchets are seen in fig. 2.

Sometimes the teeth become reduced so that the chaeta appears to be simple-pointed, occasionally with a trace of the reduced tooth visible as in *Clitellio arenarius* (fig. 10*d*). Others again are clearly simple-pointed with no trace of any teeth (dorsal bundles of *Nais alpina* for instance, fig. 5*f*).

In the Enchytraeidae the chaetae are broad, practically always simple-ended, and usually numerous, radiating fanwise, and are similar in the dorsal and ventral bundles, whereas in the Naididae and Tubificidae such uniformity is less common.

Pectinate chaetae are typical of the dorsal anterior bundles of many Tubificidae. These are essentially bifid crotchets with a series of fine intermediate teeth between the two usual teeth. The intermediate spines may be as large as the outer teeth, e.g. in *Psammorycides barbatus* and *Tubifex costatus* (figs. 8*f*, 10*c*) so that the chaeta has a broad palmate distal end.

Genital chaetae are associated with the spermathecal or penial pores in many Naididae and Tubificidae. They are frequently used in identifying Tubificidae, where the spermathecal pores are found on segment X and the male pores on segment XI (the chaetae therefore being those of the ninth and tenth ventral bundles respectively) in all but a few species to which specific reference is given in the key.

Chaetae other than hair chaetae usually have a more or less median swelling called the *nodulus*.

The following are the commonest combinations of chaetae found in the various families:

Aeolosomatidae
Hair chaetae in both dorsal and ventral bundles of all species, a single bifid crotchet in mid and posterior bundles of *Aeolosoma tenebrarum* and in *A. beddardi*.

Naididae
Either ventral chaetae only (*Chaetogaster*);
or dorsal and ventral bundles with bifid crotchets only;
or dorsal bundles with crotchets and hair chaetae, ventrals with crotchets;
or dorsal bundles with one simple chaeta per bundle, ventrals bifid crotchets (*Ophidonais serpentina*).

Tubificidae
Either dorsal and ventral bundles with bifid crotchets only;
or dorsal bundles (at least anteriorly) with hair chaetae and pectinate chaetae, ventrals bifid;
or dorsal bundles with hair chaetae, dorsal and ventral bundles with bifid crotchets.

ENCHYTRAEIDAE   All bundles with broad, simple-ended chaetae.

LUMBRICULIDAE}
DORYDRILIDAE }   2 chaetae in each bundle, usually indistinctly
                     bifid with the upper tooth reduced, or simple-
                     pointed.

GLOSSOSCOLECIDAE}
LUMBRICIDAE   }   2 chaetae per bundle, simple-pointed.

HAPLOTAXIDAE   1 chaeta per bundle, sickle-shaped; the ventral
                     chaetae are much larger than the dorsals which
                     may be absent in most posterior segments.

BRANCHIOBDELLIDAE Chaetae absent; a few toothed plates.

ECOLOGY

As these worms have been virtually ignored by ecologists, very little information is available about their geographical distribution and habitats. My own collections of Tubificidae are the chief source of information concerning this family since the records summarised by Southern (1909). There is almost no field information concerning the occurrence of Aeolosomatidae, and the ecological notes on the Naididae are mostly restricted to the bare fact that they are fresh-water or brackish water species. Comments on the habitats and distribution of British species are only inserted where there is some reliable information. Vice-comital distribution maps are not included for the same reason, but also because most species are in fact cosmopolitan, and such records may be less significant than in other groups.

The terms 'common', 'rare' and 'local' are used to indicate the number of localities at which a species may be found. The frequency of occurrence of individuals within these localities is described by 'abundant', 'frequent' or 'scarce'. Where there is only a single record of a species, a reference to the locality is given. It should not be inferred from this that the species is restricted to this one locality, but rather that our knowledge of the distribution of British Oligochaeta is sadly inadequate. For this reason the author will always be pleased to receive information (supported by specimens wherever possible) concerning occurrences of aquatic worms.

One or two species not yet recorded from Britain are included in the key to the Naididae, where to do so completes the genus as known from Europe, or they are extremely simple to key out. They will

be found in parentheses.   Where several European species of a genus
remain unrecorded a statement as to the number involved will be
found at the end of the section of the key that refers to the genus.
No non-British species of Tubificidae are included, keys to all species
being available elsewhere (Brinkhurst & Jamieson, 1971).

KEY TO FAMILIES

As with all such keys, the separation of worms into families is much easier than the diagnostic characters would suggest. They become obvious with very little experience.

1 Chaetae absent. Ectoparasitic on crayfish—
                                            BRANCHIOBDELLIDAE, p. 50

— Chaetae present, or if absent (*Achaeta,* Enchytraeidae) then worm free-living—   **2**

2 More than 2 chaetae per bundle; hair chaetae present or absent. Worms usually less than 3 dm long—   **3**

— 1 or 2 chaetae per bundle (rarely 4 when replacement chaetae are developing); no hair chaetae. Worms mostly more than 3 cm long—   **5**

3 Hair chaetae in both dorsal and ventral bundles. Worms less than 10 mm long. Prostomium ciliated. Prominent oil droplets in most species—   **AEOLOSOMATIDAE,** p. 14

— Hair chaetae in dorsal bundles only or absent. Usually more than 10 mm long. Prostomium not ciliated. No prominent oil droplets—   **4**

4 Asexual reproduction forming chains of individuals. More or less transparent. Spermathecae in segment V; male pores on segment VI (or reproductive organs duplicated by one or two segments anteriad or posteriad). Usually less than 2 cm long. Some species with eyes. Pectinate chaetae never present—
                                              NAIDIDAE, p. 17

—   Asexual reproduction uncommon, never forming chains of individuals. Spermathecae in segment X; male pores on segment XI (unless displaced by one or two segments). Usually longer than 2 cm. Most species red and coiling tightly when disturbed. No eyes. All types of chaetae present—

TUBIFICIDAE, p. 29

—   No asexual reproduction. Spermathecal pores on segment V; male pores on segment XII. Of similar size to Tubificidae but whitish-pink, and mostly terrestrial in habit. No eyes. Chaetae usually straight and broad with a simple tip (but absent in *Achaeta* and bifid in *Propappus*)—

ENCHYTRAEIDAE, p. 44

5 (2)* Chaetae 1 per bundle; the dorsal chaetae frequently absent in posterior segments, and when present much smaller than the ventrals. Very long, thread-like worms—

HAPLOTAXIDAE, p. 50

—   Chaetae 2 per bundle, all alike—   **6**

6   Small worms, mostly 10–40 mm long and less than 3 mm broad. Body more or less transparent when alive, so that the internal organs and blood vessels are readily visible. The blood vessels make the worms bright red in colour. Male genital pores usually on segment X, but may be more anterior where regeneration has occurred—   {**LUMBRICULIDAE**, p. 44

{ **DORYDRILIDAE**, p. 44

—   Much larger and thicker worms, *i.e.* the familiar earthworms and their relatives. Body wall thick and muscular so that the internal organs are invisible and the worms are pink in colour. Male pores more posterior in position—   **7**

7   Worms 80–100 mm long. Male pores minute, on segment XVII. Clitellum extending from segments XV to XXV at most. Prostomium not separated from peristomium by a groove—

GLOSSOSCOLECIDAE, p. 49
Sparganophilus tamesis Benham

* Where a key couplet is not reached from the preceding one, the number of the couplet from which the direction came is indicated thus in parentheses.

— Worms variable in size (most terrestrial). Clitellum mostly posterior to segment XXIII in all except two varieties of *Eiseniella tetraedra*. Male pores on segment XV (XIII in *E. tetraedra* var. *macrura*)— **LUMBRICIDAE**, p. 51

Eiseniella tetraedra is the only lumbricid commonly met in fresh water and is easily recognised as it is square in section posteriorly.

— Large worms, 120–320 × 3–5 mm. Male pores prominent on segment XV. Body trapezoidal in cross-section, with the upper surface broader than the lower. Spermathecae absent—

GLOSSOSCOLECIDAE,
Criodrilus lacuum Hoffm.
(Not recorded from Britain)

KEYS TO SPECIES

Family AEOLOSOMATIDAE

Only one genus of this family, *Aeolosoma*, has been recorded in Britain. The worms are very small, and for this reason are usually found only in aquaria although probably abundant in nature; hence they are poorly known. See Burke (1967) and Brinkhurst & Jamieson (1971).

1 Hair chaetae and crotchets present, at least in posterior bundles—   2

— Hair chaetae only in both dorsal and ventral bundles—   3

2 Worms 5–10 mm long. Anterior bundles containing about 3 long and 1 short hair chaetae; mid- and posterior bundles containing about 3 hair chaetae and 1 bifid crotchet. Droplets yellow-olive green. (Prostomium pointed, wider than the succeeding segments)— **Aeolosoma tenebrarum** Vejdovsky

— Worms 1–2·5 mm long. Hair chaetae S-shaped, all the same length, anteriorly 3–4, posteriorly 2 per bundle; crotchets present. Droplets colourless. (Prostomium wider than succeeding segments)— **Aeolosoma beddardi** Michaelsen

A. beddardi Mich. differs from *A. niveum* Leydig (the only other European species — Ude 1929) in that the characteristic orange oil droplets are missing.

3 (1) Droplets orange or red— 4

— Droplets colourless or green— 5

4 Worms 1–5 mm long. Prostomium twice as wide as the succeeding segments. Hair chaetae straight, 3–5 long and 3–5 short ones in each bundle—
Aeolosoma hemprichi Ehrenberg

— Worms very short (no figures available). Prostomium equal to body in width. Hair chaetae S-shaped, all of one length, 3 per bundle— **Aeolosoma quaternarium** Ehrenberg

5 (3) Worms 1·5–4 mm long. Hair chaetae sharply bent, long and short in the same bundle, 3–4 per bundle. Droplets colourless or bright green— **Aeolosoma variegatum** Vejdovsky

— Worms 1–2 mm long. Hair chaetae described by Beddard as of the same shape as those of *A. variegatum,* but drawn almost straight in his figure, 3–6 per bundle. Droplets colourless or greenish blue— **Aeolosoma headleyi** Beddard

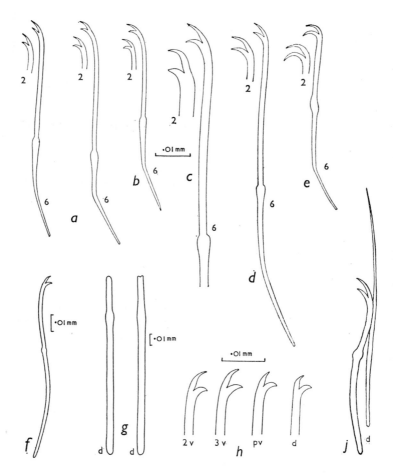

Fig. 2. Chaetae of Naididae:

 a, *Chaetogaster diastrophus;*
 b, *C. langi;*
 c, *C. diaphanus;*
 d, *C. cristallinus;*
 e, *C. limnaei;*

 f, *Uncinais uncinata;*
 g, *Ophidonais serpentina;*
 h, *Paranais litoralis;*
 j, *Haemonais waldvogeli.*

Numbers refer to segments; p, posterior; d, dorsal; v, ventral.

Family NAIDIDAE

The following key has been modified from Sperber's (1950) key to the European species. All the figures of chaetae are based on her original drawings, kindly lent to the author.

1 Ventral chaetae only, the dorsal bundles absent—
genus CHAETOGASTER, 2

— Dorsal and ventral chaetae present— 6

2 Commensal with gastropod snails,living in the mantle cavity and kidney. Chaetae numerous, with long, curved teeth (fig. 2e)—
Chaetogaster limnaei Von Baer

Probably common; several specimens were found on each snail examined from ponds in the Wirral (Cheshire).

— Free-living— 3

3 Worms 2·5–7 mm or even 25 mm long. Longest chaetae of segment II at least 140μ long— 4

— Worms 0·5–5 mm long. Longest chaetae of segment II less than 125μ long— 5

4 Worms up to 25 mm long, very transparent. Longest chaetae of segment II usually longer than 200μ (fig. 2c)—
Chaetogaster diaphanus (Gruithuisen)

Fresh and brackish water. Rivers and ponds; England and Scotland.

— Worms up to 7 mm long. Longest chaetae of segment II 140–165μ long (fig. 2d)—
Chaetogaster cristallinus Vejdovsky

Fresh and brackish water. England, Scotland and Ireland.

5 (3) Prostomium pointed.   Chaetae curved through a rather small
angle at the tip, and with the teeth only slightly divergent
(fig. 2a)—   **Chaetogaster diastrophus** (Gruithuisen)

Known from Ireland and Oxford.

— Prostomium obtuse.   Chaetae curved through a larger angle at
the tip, and with the teeth more divergent (fig. 2b)—
Chaetogaster langi Bretscher
Known only from Scotland.

6 (1) Dorsal bundles containing bifid crotchets only—   7

— Dorsal bundles containing crotchets and hair chaetae—   8

— Dorsal bundles consisting of a single simple-ended broad chaeta
(fig. 2g)—   **Ophidonais serpentina** (Müller)

R. Birkett, Leasowe (Cheshire); Shropshire Union Canal (Shropshire); Oxwich Marsh (Glamorgan); Cambridge; Ireland.

7 Dorsal chaetae beginning in segment VI. Eyes present*.
(Chaetae as in fig. 2f)—   **Uncinais uncinata** (Ørstedt)

Fresh and brackish water.   Malham Tarn (mid-Yorkshire).

— Dorsal chaetae beginning in segment II; 4–12 simple crotchets
per bundle.   No eyes—   **Homochaeta naidina** Bretscher

In a stony riffle in R. Severn at Montford Bridge (Shropshire);
R. Wharfe (Yorkshire).
    H. setosa (Moszynski), a species known only from Poland, differs
from *H. naidina* in its obtuse instead of pointed anterior end.

— Dorsal chaetae beginning in segment V; (chaetae as in fig. 2h).
No eyes—   **Paranais litoralis** (Müller)

Brackish and salt water.   Sheerness (E. Kent) and Norfolk.

Three species of *Paranais*, *P. friči* Hrabě, *P. botniensis* Sperber
and *P. simplex* Hrabě have not yet been recorded from Britain.

* Recent work on Italian material shows that eyeless worms may also be found in
this species.

8 (6) Dorsal chaetae beginning in segment II— genus PRISTINA. **9**

—   Dorsal chaetae beginning in segment IV, V or VI—   **13**

—   Dorsal chaetae beginning in segment XVIII, XIX or XX; (chaetae as in fig. 2*j*)—   **Haemonais waldvogeli** Bretscher

       Not yet recorded in Britain.

9   Proboscis absent—   **10**

—   Proboscis present (fig. 3*i*⁄)—   **11**

10 Dorsal chaetae stout, the upper tooth weak or absent; posterior ventral chaetae with the upper tooth shorter than the lower (fig. 3*b*)—   **Pristina menoni** (Aiyer)

    Two stony streams in N. Wales.

—   Dorsal chaetae with long parallel teeth (fig. 3*e*d); posterior ventral chaetae with teeth of about equal length (fig. 3*e*pv)—
                                    Pristina idrensis Sperber
    Stony stream in N. Wales.

11 (9) Dorsal crotchets simple pointed (fig. 3*g*d); elongate hair chaetae (fig. 3*g*h) on segment III; (ventral chaetae simple bifid crotchets with the upper tooth thinner and a little longer than the lower, fig. 3*g*av)—   **Pristina longiseta** Ehrenberg

    Ascog (Bute).

—   Dorsal crotchets bifid; no elongate hair chaetae—   **12**

12 Ventral chaetae behind segment VII (fig. 3*h* 7, 8v) stouter and more curved than the anterior ones; enlarged chaetae with a long distal tooth (fig. 3*h* 4v) usually present in segment IV or V or both; (dorsal chaetae straight with small teeth fig. 3*h* d)—
                                    Pristina aequiseta Bourne

    Botanic Gardens, Regent's Park.

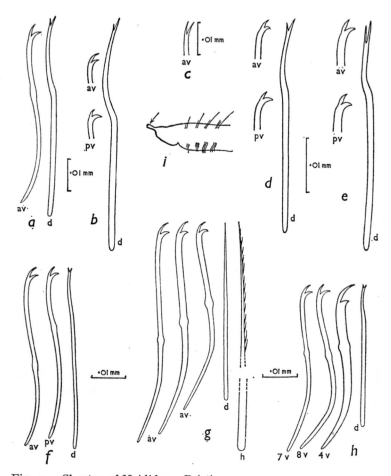

Fig. 3.   Chaetae of Naididae—*Pristina* :

a, *Pristina rosea;*
b, *P. menoni;*
c, *P. bilobata;*
d, *P. amphibiotica;*
e, *P. idrensis;*

f, *P. foreli;*
g, *P. longiseta;*
h, *P. aequiseta;*
i, *Pristina* to illustrate
       proboscis.

a, anterior; p, posterior; d, dorsal; v, ventral; h, hair chaetae;
4v, enlarged ventral chaeta of segment IV; (numbers refer to
segments).

— Ventral chaetae all of one type, with thin, more or less equal teeth (fig. 3*f*)— **Pristina foreli** Piguet

Oakmere (Cheshire).

Three further European species, *P. rosea* (Piguet), *P. bilobata* (Bretscher) and *P. amphibiotica* Lastočkin, have not yet been recorded in Britain. Their chaetae are shown in fig. 3*a*, *c*, d.

13 (8) Gills present at the posterior end (fig. 4*a*, *c* pg)— **14**

— Gills absent— **16**

14 Long ciliated projections associated with the gills (fig. 4*c*). Inhabits a fixed or portable tube. Ventral chaetae with strongly curved teeth, dorsal chaetae with a short upper tooth (fig. 4*c*)— **Aulophorus furcatus** (Müller)

Kew Gardens (Surrey).

— No elongate ciliated projections associated with the gills (fig. 4*a*). Tube-dwelling— genus DERO, **15**

15 One small dorsal pair and three ventral, foliate pairs of gills (fig. 4*a* pg). A single crotchet in each dorsal bundle, with the upper tooth longer than the lower (fig. 4*a* d); anterior ventral chaetae with thin teeth, posterior ventral chaetae with thicker, shorter teeth (fig. 4*a* av, pv)— **Dero digitata** (Müller)

Tube-dwelling. Windermere (Westmorland) and Kew Gardens (Surrey).

— Two ventral and one lateral pairs of gills. A single crotchet in each dorsal bundle, with the teeth equal in length (fig. 4*b* d); anterior ventral chaetae with extremely thin teeth, posterior ventral chaetae with very short teeth (fig. 4*b* av, pv)— **Dero obtusa** Udekem

Tube-dwelling. Pond on the Wirral (Cheshire) and Kew Gardens (Surrey).

Two further European species, *Dero dorsalis* Ferronière and *D. nivea* Aiyer, have not yet been recorded from Britain.

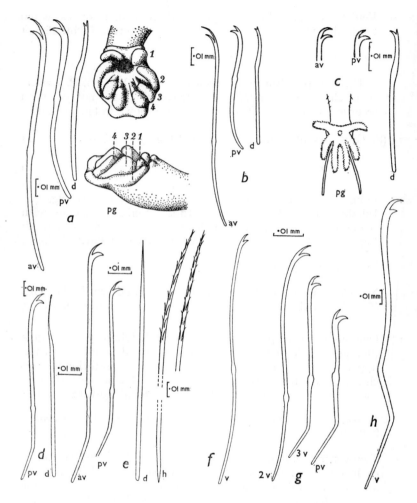

Fig. 4.   Chaetae and gills of Naididae:

a, *Dero digitata;*
b, *D. obtusa;*
c, *Aulophorus furcatus;*
d, *Slavina appendiculata;*

e, *Vejdovskyella comata;*
f, *Arcteonais lomondi;*
g, *Ripistes parasita;*
h, *Stylaria lacustris.*

Numbers refer to segments; a, anterior; p, posterior; d, dorsal;
v, ventral; pg, gills at posterior end; h, hair chaetae.

16 (13) With a proboscis—   **17**

— No proboscis—   **19**

17 Dorsal bundles of segments VI to VIII containing 10–18 2–6 normal hair chaetae, and 2–16 giant hair chaetae 780–1700μ long; (ventral chaetae fig. 4g, those of segment II S-shaped, more posterior chaetae bent proximally)—
Ripistes parasita (Schmidt)

(*Paranais macrochaeta* Bourne).   Inhabits a fixed tube.

— Giant hair chaetae absent—   **18**

18 Dorsal bundles containing 8–18 hairs and 9–12 extremely thin crotchets.   Ventral chaetae slightly S-shaped (fig. 4f)—
Arcteonais lomondi (Martin)
Loch Lomond.

— Dorsal bundles containing 1–3 hairs and 3–4 simple-pointed crotchets.   Ventral chaetae twice bent (fig. 4h)—
Stylaria lacustris (Linn.)

Fresh and brackish water; common, especially in lakes.

19 (16) Hair chaetae of segment VI very long.   Body encrusted with foreign matter.   Dorsal crotchets hair-like, the tips slightly distended (fig. 4d d); (ventral crotchets simply bifid, bent proximally, as fig. 4d pv)— **Slavina appendiculata** (Udekem)

Known only from Ascog (Bute).

— No elongate hair chaetae. Body not encrusted. Dorsal crotchets simple-pointed or bifid—   **20**

20 Hair chaetae strongly serrated (fig. 4e h); dorsal crotchets simple-pointed (fig. 4e d); (ventral crotchets simply bifid, bent proximally as fig. 4e av, pv)—
Vejdovskyella comata (Vejdovsky)

In a hill stream in N. Wales, Ascog (Bute), and Ireland.

Another species, *V. intermedia* (Bretscher), has not yet been recorded from Britain.

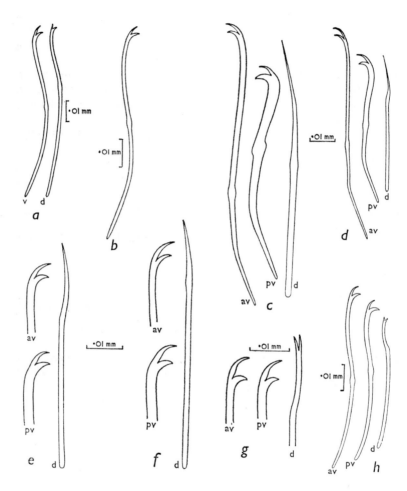

Fig. 5.   Chaetae of Naididae:

a, *Specaria josinae;*   e, *N. simplex;*
b, *Piguetiella blanci;*   f, *N. alpina;*
c, *Nais barbata;*   g, *N. elinguis;*
d, *N. pseudobtusa;*   h, *N. communis.*

d, dorsal; v, ventral; a, anterior; p. posterior.

—   Hair chaetae smooth, without serrations—   **21**

21   No eyes.   Dorsal bundles containing 2–6 hair chaetae and 2–6
     crotchets with about equal teeth (fig. 5a d); ventral bundles with
     5–10 chaetae, all alike, with the upper tooth a little longer than
     the lower (fig. 5a v)—   **Specaria josinae** (Vejdovsky)

     Esthwaite Water (Lancashire).

—   Usually no eyes.   Chaetae fewer—   **22**

22   Dorsal and ventral crotchets alike, bifid with equal teeth
     (fig. 5b); dorsal bundles containing 2–3 crotchets and 0–3 hair
     chaetae less than twice as long as the crotchets—
                                        Piguetiella blanci (Piguet)

     One doubtful record from Windermere.

—   Dorsal and ventral crotchets differing, the dorsal either simple-
     pointed or with two more or less parallel teeth, ventral chaetae
     bifid; hair chaetae 1–3, seldom 4 or 5 per bundle, usually more
     than twice as long as the crotchets—   genus NAIS, **23**

23   Dorsal crotchets simple-pointed—   **24**

—   Dorsal crotchets bifid—   **27**

24   Tips of dorsal crotchets long and sharp (fig. 5c, d d)—   **25**

—   Tips of dorsal crotchets obtuse (fig. 5e, f d)—   **26**

25   Ventral chaetae with teeth of equal length, those posterior to
     segment V shorter, stouter and more curved than those of the
     more anterior segments (fig. 5c av, pv); dorsal bundles containing
     up to 5 hair chaetae and 5 needle-like crotchets (fig. 5c d)—
                                            Nais barbata (Müller)

     Derby; Cavendish Dock, Barrow (Lancashire); and Ireland.

— Ventral chaetae posterior to segment V thin and straight, with the upper tooth $1\frac{1}{2}$ times as long as the lower (fig. 5*d* av, pv); dorsal bundles containing 1–3 hair chaetae and 1–3 short, needle-like crotchets (fig. 5*d* d)—   **Nais pseudobtusa** Piguet

Edinburgh; ? Isle of Man.

26 (24) Ventral chaetae all alike, the upper tooth twice as long as the lower (fig. 5*f*)—   **Nais alpina** Sperber

In hill streams. Afon Hirnant (Merioneth), common in moss.

— Anterior ventral chaetae with the upper tooth longer than the lower (fig. 5*e* av), posterior with equal teeth (fig. 5*e* pv)—
   Nais simplex Piguet
Ascog (Bute), Reading (Berkshire).

27 (23) Ventral chaetae behind segment V partly very stout, with the distal tooth several times as long as the proximal (fig. 6)—
   28

— Ventral chaetae all of similar size—   29

28 Thick ventral chaetae beginning in segment VII; in some segments there are giant chaetae with reduced proximal teeth (fig. 6*a*)—   **Nais bretscheri** Michaelsen

R. Eden, Carlisle; R. Derwent below Derby; East Stoke (Dorset).

— Thick ventral chaetae beginning in segment VI; giant chaetae absent (fig. 6*b*)—   **Nais pardalis** Piguet

A doubtful record from Dorset; R. Nene at Northampton and Peterborough.

Specimens of *N. pardalis* without thickened chaetae are difficult to separate from *N. variabilis*. The hair chaetae are 100–200µ long in the former, but often 300–500µ long in the latter. The ventral chaetae of *N. bretscheri* and *N. pardalis* are very variable in form, as indicated in fig. 6.

29 (27) Dorsal crotchets with long, almost parallel, teeth. All ventral chaetae with the upper tooth twice as long as the lower (fig. 5*g*)— **Nais elinguis** Müller

Common and abundant in polluted water; also in brackish water. Mostly in rivers, but also known from Oakmere (Cheshire).

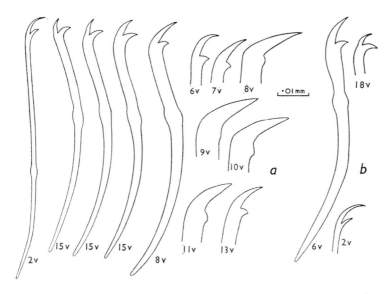

Fig. 6. Chaetae of Naididae:

  a, Nais bretscheri; 2v, 15v, normal ventral chaetae; 8v, thick ventral chaeta from segment VIII of a specimen with no giant chaetae; 6v, 7v, 13v, thick ventral chaetae from a specimen with giant chaetae; 9–11 v, giant ventral chaetae.

  b, Nais pardalis; 2v, 18v, normal ventral chaetae; 6v, thickened ventral chaeta.

— Dorsal crotchets with teeth short and diverging; posterior ventral crotchets with teeth equally long— **30**

30 Eyes sometimes absent.   Anterior ventral chaetae with the
    upper tooth about twice as long as the lower—
                                     Nais variabilis Piguet
    Fresh and brackish water.   Ascog (Bute) and Edinburgh.
      See note on *N. pardalis* in couplet 28.

—   Eyes present.   Anterior ventral chaetae thinner, longer and
    straighter than the posterior chaetae, but the teeth equally long
    in both (fig. 5*h*)—   **Nais communis** Piguet

    Fresh and brackish water.   Hayes (Middlesex); Trawsfynydd
    (Merioneth); Glamorgan; Duddingston (Midlothian); Co. Clare.

    One east-European species, *N. behningi* Michaelsen, has not
    been recorded in Britain.

Family TUBIFICIDAE

The genera in this family may be determined from the form of the male efferent ducts (fig. 7). Since, however, most species may be determined from their chaetae alone, these characters are not used in this key. Keys to all the species of the family are given by Brinkhurst (1963a).

1 Hair chaetae present—   2

— Hair chaetae absent—   16

2 Posterior segments bearing gill filaments (fig. 8b). Dorsal bundles containing 1–3 short hair chaetae and 11–12 crotchets (some with a few short spines between the teeth of the anterior dorsal crotchets); ventral bundles containing 10–11 crotchets; all crotchets with reduced upper teeth (fig. 8a)—
Branchiura sowerbyi Beddard

Usually in warm water tanks in botanical gardens, or in warm effluents, *e.g.* R. Thames at Reading (Berkshire), but occasionally in rivers of normal temperature.

— No gill filaments—   3

3 Body wall more or less beset with small papillae (Pl. 1, *A*).* Hair chaetae broad and short—   genus PELOSCOLEX, 4

— Body wall covered by a simple, thin cuticle without such papillae (Pl. 1, *B*). Hair chaetae long and thin—   6

---

* See footnote on p. 31.

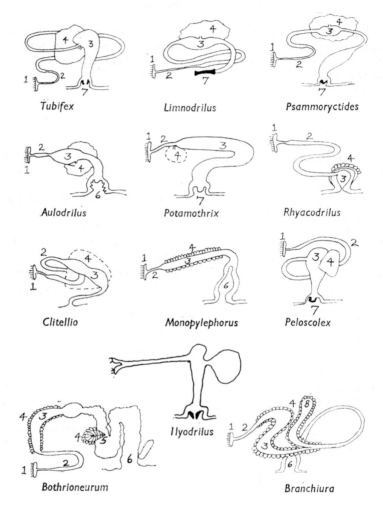

Fig. 7.   Diagram of the male efferent ducts of one side of segment XI
of the commoner genera of the Tubificidae to show the principal
generic characters.   Broken outlines indicate organs that are
absent in some species.   1, sperm funnel; 2, vas deferens;
3, atrium; 4, prostate gland; 5, paratrium; 6, pseudopenis;
7, penis; 8, diverticulum.

4 Hair chaetae few or none; (both dorsal and ventral bundles usually containing 2 crotchets with much reduced upper teeth — fig. 8c). Papillae few and discrete. Common and frequent in brackish water—   **Peloscolex benedeni** (Udekem)

— Hair chaetae present in dorsal bundles. Papillae so numerous as to obscure the body wall between them.* Fresh water— **5**

5 Dorsal bundles containing about 5 pectinate crotchets (fig. 8d pt) and about 7 hair chaetae; ventral crotchets strongly bifid, with broad lower teeth (fig. 8d v)—   **Peloscolex ferox** (Eisen)

Scarce in rivers; more abundant in lakes.

— Dorsal bundles containing 1–4 hair chaetae and 4 short, hair-like crotchets; ventral crotchets all more or less simple-pointed (fig. 8e)—   **Peloscolex velutinus** (Grube)

Single specimens from R. Ouzel (Bedfordshire), a stream at Raynards Park, Cranleigh (Surrey); and the R. Thames, Reading (Berkshire).

6 (3) Dorsal bundles containing 6–7 hair chaetae and 8–10 crotchets; ventral bundles containing up to 10 crotchets; the upper tooth of all crotchets shorter and thinner than the lower (fig. 8h). Spermathecal and male pores paired—
                    Aulodrilus pluriseta (Piguet)

Common in lakes, rivers, canals and ponds; sometimes abundant.

---

* Some specimens may be found without the papillae, which appear to be shed periodically. The chaetae are however sufficiently distinct to make identification possible.

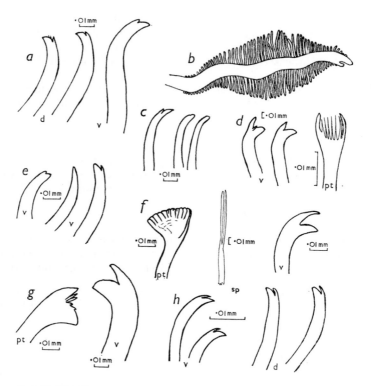

Fig. 8.   Tubificidae:

a, *Branchiura sowerbyi*;

b, *B. sowerbyi* — posterior end with dorsal and ventral gill filaments;

c, *Peloscolex benedeni*;

d. *P. ferox*;

e, *P. velutinus*;

f, *Psammoryctides barbatus*;

g, *P. albicola*;

h, *Aulodrilus pluriseta*.

d, dorsal; v, ventral; pt, pectinate; sp, spermathecal.

— Dorsal bundles containing 0–2 hair chaetae, characteristically twisted distally, and 3–4 crotchets occasionally with a small intermediate tooth; ventral bundles with 3–4 crotchets. Spermathecal and male pores single, mid-ventral—
Monopylephorus irroratus (Verrill)
(*Postiodrilus sonderi* Boldt)

Usually marine littoral; recently obtained from the saline R. Weaver (Cheshire).

— Chaetae fewer in each bundle and not of this form, the dorsal crotchets always pectinate. Spermathecal and male pores paired—   7

7   Anterior dorsal bundles containing 7–8 crotchets, all broad and palmate (fig. 8*f* pt). Spermathecal chaetae thin, straight and hollow ended (fig. 8*f* sp); ventral crotchets strongly bifid (fig. 8*f* v)—   **Psammoryctides barbatus** (Grube)

Rivers and ponds, occasionally where polluted; common and frequent.

— Anterior dorsal crotchets pectinate, with prominent lateral teeth and a series of fine intermediate spines (figs. 8, 9 pt)—   8

8   Anterior dorsal crotchets 1–3 per bundle, thick, with the upper tooth short and much thinner than the broad, curved lower tooth and very few intermediate spines between the lateral teeth (fig. 8*g* pt). Spermathecal chaetae present as in *P. barbatus* (fig. 8*f* sp)— **Psammoryctides albicola** (Michaelsen)

Rare and scarce.   R. Thames, Reading (Berkshire); Tillgate Brook (W. Essex); R. Wharfe (Yorkshire); one very doubtful record from Windermere.

— Chaetae not of this form.   Dorsal pectinate chaetae with more or less equal lateral teeth, intermediate spines markedly thinner than lateral teeth—   9

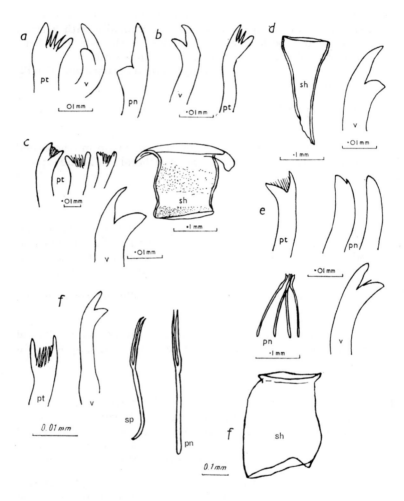

Fig. 9.   Chaetae and penis sheaths of *Tubifex, Ilyodrilus, Rhyacodrilus*
          and *Peloscolex*:

a, *Tubifex nerthus;*   d, *Ilyodrilus templetoni;*
b, *T. ignotus;*   e, *Rhyacodrilus coccineus.*
c, *T. tubifex;*   f, *Peloscolex speciosus.*

pn, penial; pt, dorsal pectinate; sh, cuticular penis sheath;
v, anterior ventral; sp, spermathecal.

9   Anterior dorsal crotchets small and thin, with the lateral teeth equal in size forming a U-shaped tip, with a few well defined intermediate spines (fig. 9*a*, *b* pt)—   **10**

—   Anterior dorsal crotchets larger, with a series of intermediate spines (figs. 9*e*, 10 pt)—   **11**

10 Worms not markedly thin. No elongate hair chaetae. Anterior ventral chaetae (fig. 9*a* v) with the upper tooth much longer and thinner than the lower; the lower tooth becoming progressively reduced in successive posterior bundles until it is very thin or absent in the penial chaetae (fig. 9*a* pn). Ventral bundles mostly of 4 chaetae—   **Tubifex nerthus** Michaelsen

Brackish water. Silverburn, Castletown (Isle of Man).

—   Worms exceptionally thin. Very elongate hair chaetae on some segments, especially just behind the clitellum. Anterior ventral chaetae 3–4 per bundle, with the upper tooth thinner but not much longer than the lower (fig. 9*b* v). No modified penial chaetae—   **Tubifex ignotus** (Štolc)

Rivers, local and scarce. R. Thames, Reading (Berkshire); R. Clwyd, Pont David (Flintshire); Silverburn, Ballasalla (Isle of Man); Loughrigg Tarn (Westmorland); R. Ribble, Halton (Yorkshire); Kenfig Pool (Glamorgan).

11 (9) Pectinate chaetae lyre-shaped (fig. 9*f*). Penial and spermathecal chaetae long, straight, hollow topped. Short cylindrical penis sheaths present—   **Peloscolex speciosus** (Hrabĕ)

(*Peloscolex simsi* Brinkhurst) R. Frome, E. Stoke.

—   Never with penis sheaths, penial and spermathecal setae modified in the same species—   **12**

*12 Anterior dorsal crotchets straight proximal to the nodulus; teeth equal in length and divergent, with a series of fine intermediate spines (fig. 9*e* pt). Penial chaetae simple-pointed and characteristically grouped (fig. 9*e* pn). (Anterior dorsal bundles with about 5 crotchets and 3–5 hair chaetae)—
                          Rhyacodrilus coccineus (Vejdovsky)

Common and abundant, often in sandy reaches of rivers.

—   Crochets more sigmoid; penial chaetae unmodified—   **13**

* From this point to couplet 15 only mature specimens can be identified with certainty.

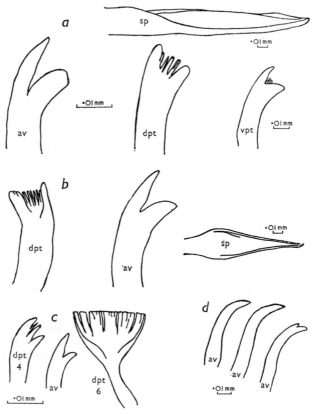

Fig. 10. Chaetae of Tubificidae:

a, *Potamothrix hammoniensis;*   c, *Tubifex costatus;*
b, *P. bavaricus;*   d, *Clitellio arenarius.*

a, anterior; d, dorsal; v, ventral; pt, pectinate; sp, spermathecal; numbers refer to segments.

13 Penes with a cuticular sheath (figs. 9c, d sh). No specially
modified genital chaetae—   **14**

—   Penes without a cuticular sheath. Spermathecal chaetae
modified—   **15**

14 Penes with short, tub-like sheaths (fig. 9c sh). (Dorsal bundles
containing 1–4 hair chaetae and 3–5 pectinate chaetae fig. 9c pt.)
Anterior ventral bundles containing 4–6 crotchets with the
upper tooth much thinner but no longer than the lower, rarely
with small intermediate spines (fig. 9c v)—
                                      Tubifex tubifex (Müller)

Common and abundant everywhere, very often with *Limnodrilus
hoffmeisteri*, especially in organically polluted waters, where they
may reach very large numbers in the absence of leeches.

—   Penes with elongate sheaths (fig. 9d sh). (Dorsal chaetae as
above). Anterior ventral bundles containing 3–4 crotchets with
the upper tooth thinner and much longer than the lower
(fig. 9d v)—   **Ilyodrilus templetoni** (Southern)
(*Tubifex templetoni* Southern)

Scarce. R. Birkett, Fornalls Green, Wirral, Rostherne Mere
(Cheshire); Windermere and Elterwater (Westmorland).

15 (13) Spermathecal chaetae long and narrow (fig. 10a sp).
Anterior dorsal bundles containing 3–5 hair chaetae and 3–5
pectinate chaetae (fig. 10a dpt); in ventral bundles 3–6 crotchets
which occasionally have small intermediate spines (fig. 10a av,
vpt)—   **Potamothrix hammoniensis** (Michaelsen)
(*Euilyodrilus hammoniensis* (Michaelsen))

Common and abundant in rivers, lakes and ponds.

—   Spermathecal chaetae short and broad (fig. 10b sp). Dorsal
bundles containing 1–5 hair chaetae and 2–5 pectinate chaetae
(fig. 10b dpt); in ventral bundles 3–4 crotchets (fig. 10b av)—
                          Potamothrix bavaricus (Oschmann)
(*Euilyodrilus bavaricus* (Oschmann))

Rare and scarce.

A form with the genital pores more anterior than usual has been
described as *P. bedoti* (Piguet) but is doubtfully distinct from
P. bavaricus (Brinkhurst 1963a).

16 (1) Body covered with papillae.   Dorsal and ventral bundles
mostly containing 2 more or less simple crotchets (fig. 8c), but
dorsal bundles may include up to 2 hair chaetae (see couplet 4,
p. 31)—   **Peloscolex benedeni** (Udekem)
Brackish water.

— No papillae, except on the clitellum of mature worms—   **17**

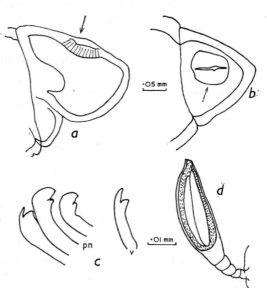

Fig. 11.   *Bothrioneurum vejdovskyanum:*
          a, b, prostomial pit (*a,* lateral; *b,* dorsal view);
          c, chaetae, (v, anterior ventral, pn, penial);
          d, spermatophore attached to the body-wall.

17   Anterior dorsal bundles of segments V to XII, XIII or XIV
containing 5–11 broad palmate chaetae (fig. 10c dpt 6).   Dorsal
chaetae of segments II to V may be somewhat intermediate
between bifid crotchets and palmate chaetae as in fig. 10c dpt 4.
Ventral chaetae as in fig. 10c av, with the upper tooth longer
and thinner than the lower—   **Tubifex costatus** Claparède
Local and abundant in brackish water.

— Anterior dorsal chaetae simple or bifid crotchets—   **18**

18 Chaetae all more or less simple-pointed or with reduced upper
teeth (fig. 10*d*). (Brackish water or on the sea shore.)— **28**

— Chaetae all bifid crotchets with the upper tooth as long as or
longer than the lower in almost all instances. Usually fresh
water; some brackish— **19**

19* Prostomium with a pronounced pit (fig. 11*a, b↗*). (Chaetae
2–5 per bundle, simple (fig. 11*c* v); penial chaetae modified
(fig. 11*c* pn)). No spermathecae; spermatophores attached to
the body wall in the genital region (fig. 11*d*)—
Bothrioneurum vejdovskyanum Štolc

R. Derwent (Derbyshire).

— No prostomial pit. Spermathecae present. (No modified
penial chaetae.)— **20**

20 Penes with cuticular sheaths (fig. 12 sh)— **21**

— No cuticular penis-sheaths— **26**

21 Penis-sheaths almost always >5 times longer than broad, and
invariably with an elaborate hood at the distal end (figs. 12*b,
c, e*)— **22**

— Penis-sheaths not >5 times longer than broad, and without an
elaborate hood at the distal end (fig. 12*d, f* sh)— **23**

* From this point onwards most species can only be certainly identified as mature
specimens.

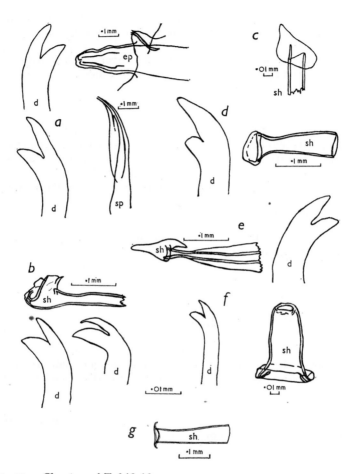

Fig. 12.   Chaetae of Tubificidae:

a, *Euilyodrilus moldaviensis;*	d, *L. udekemianus;*
b, *Limnodrilus hoffmeisteri*	e, *L. cervix;*
(including a ventral chaeta	f, *Tubifex pseudogaster;*
of the 'parvus' type);	g, *Limnodrilus*
c, *L. claparedeianus;*	*profundicola.*

d, anterior dorsal; pn, penial; sp. spermathecal chaetae;
ep, everted penis; sh, cuticular penis sheath.

22 Penis-sheaths usually 20–30 times longer than broad, with a very thick wall which narrows abruptly just before the distal end (fig. 12*e* sh); distal hood with the shape of two triangles in line with the axis of the penis, one pointing forward and one back. Up to 10 chaetae per bundle, with the upper tooth a little longer and thinner than the lower (fig. 12*e* d)—

Limnodrilus cervix Brinkhurst

R. Thames, Reading (Berkshire); Shropshire Union Canal, Chester, and several other canals. Named *L. claparedeianus* in previous publications by Brinkhurst and Kennedy, but now thought to have been introduced from America (Kennedy 1965).

— Penis-sheaths as in fig. 12*c* sh, up to 30 times as long as broad but thin-walled; distal hood broadly pear shaped. Chaetae 5–7 per bundle, with the upper tooth, especially in anterior bundles, often longer than but not much thicker than the lower— **Limnodrilus claparedeianus** Ratzel

R. Thames at Reading; Shropshire Union Canal, Chester; streams in the Wirral (Cheshire); streams in the Isle of Man; R. Derwent, Derby.

— Penis-sheaths very variable in length, but most commonly some 10–20 times longer than broad (fig. 12*b* sh), the wall thin, the distal end bearing a hood of variable form usually set at right-angles to the long axis of the sheath. Chaetae 4–8 per bundle, with the upper tooth a little longer and thinner than the lower (fig. 12*b* d)— **Limnodrilus hoffmeisteri** Claparède

Fresh, rarely brackish, water; common and abundant; often with *Tubifex tubifex* in polluted water.

A form in which the upper tooth of the anterior chaetae may be shorter than the lower has been named *parvus* (Southern). This is almost certainly the effect of erosion of the teeth and therefore not a true variety (fig. 12*b* d).

23 (21) Penis-sheaths cylindrical (figs. 12*d*, *g* sh)— 24

— Penis-sheaths conical or tub-shaped (figs. 9*c*, *d*, 12*f* sh)— **25**

24 Penis-sheaths short and simple (fig. 12*d* sh). Chaetae 5–8 per bundle, the upper tooth much longer than the lower, and as thick or thicker (fig. 12*d* d)—

Limnodrilus udekemianus Claparède

Fairly common and abundant, mostly in rivers but occasionally in ponds; may occur in somewhat organically polluted water.

— Penis-sheaths 3–5 times longer than broad, usually with the
   distal end strongly reflected (fig. 12g sh). Chaetae 5–7 in
   dorsal, 4–6 in ventral bundles, the upper tooth slightly thinner
   than the lower—   **Limnodrilus profundicola** (Verrill)
   (*L. helveticus* Piguet)

> Known from only one small pond in the Wirral, Cheshire, and
> Ditton Brook (Lancs.); otherwise in Swiss lakes and rivers.

25 (23) Penis-sheaths tub-shaped (fig. 9c sh). (Chaetae 3–5 per
   bundle, with teeth equally long or the upper slightly shorter
   than the lower)—   **Tubifex newaensis** (Mich.)

> Three specimens found in the Erewash canal at the junction of the
> R. Trent and the R. Derwent, Derbyshire, are much smaller than
> the Russian specimens of this species but are otherwise identical to
> them.

   Penis-sheaths conical (fig. 12f sh). Chaetae 3–6 in dorsal,
   2–3 in ventral bundles, with the upper tooth slightly thinner
   and longer than the lower (fig. 12f d)—
                                    Tubifex pseudogaster (Dahl)

> Brackish water.   Watermouth (Devon); Isle of Man.

26 (20) Penial chaetae large, sickle shaped.
                        Rhyacodrilus falciformis Bretscher
   Llangadwaladr, Denbigh—

— Penial setae unmodified—   27

27 Spermathecal chaetae broad and elongated (fig. 12a sp).
   Spermathecal pores paired.   Penes paired and prominent
   ventro-laterally in mature specimens (fig. 12a ep).   No
   chitinous penis-sheaths.   Chaetae 7–9 or more per bundle
   (fig. 12a d)—
                  Potamothrix moldaviensis (Vejdovsky & Mràzek)
   (*Euilyodrilus moldaviensis* Vejdovsky & Mràzek)

> Locally frequent in fresh water.   R. Thames, Reading (Berkshire);
> R. Morda near Oswestry (Shropshire); R. Weaver, Shrewbridge
> and Shropshire Union Canal, Chester (Cheshire): Great Ouse,
> Bedford; Cole Mere (Shropshire).

— No modified spermathecal chaetae. Spermathecal pores united in a single mid-ventral aperture. Penes with a single median pore when fully mature. Chaetae mostly 3–5 per bundle, with the upper tooth longer and thinner than the lower; some simple-pointed chaetae may be present in posterior segments—
Monopylephorus rubroniveus (Levinsen)
(*Vermiculus pilosus* Goodrich)

Marine littoral or saline water. Mouth of R. Weaver (Cheshire); Sheerness (Kent).

28 (18) Very thin, small worms <3 cm long. Chaetae with the upper tooth thinner and much shorter than the lower— **29**

— Worms usually 3–6·5 cm long. Chaetae all more or less simple-pointed with the upper tooth much reduced (fig. 10*d*). Spermathecae paired and opening ventro-laterally on segment 10— **Clitellio arenarius** (Müller)

Common in freshets running through gravel on the sea shore.

29 Penial chaetae absent. Only one spermathecal pore on the dorsal surface of segment X. Spermatheca single (Chaetae mostly 3–4 per bundle anteriorly)—
Phallodrilus monospermathecus (Knöllner)
(*Aktedrilus monospermathecus* Knöllner)

In Britain known only from Hale (Lancashire), but probably widespread, as it is known from the Baltic to the Mediterranean in brackish and marine habitats.

— Up to 20 penial chaetae in each ventral bundle of segment 11, thicker and straighter than normal chaetae. Two spermathecae opening latero-ventrally on segment XI. (Chaetae 5–6 per bundle anteriorly; some posterior chaetae simple-pointed)—
Thalassodrilus prostatus (Knöllner)
(*Rhyacodrilus prostatus* Knöllner)

Found by Mr M. J. Tynen in the Menai Straits in seaweed buried in shingle, and sent to me by Dr T. B. Reynoldson. Probably on other shores (Brinkhurst 1963c).

Family ENCHYTRAEIDAE

Some forty of the species in this family are recorded from Britain (Brinkhurst 1962–3). The majority cannot be classified as exclusively aquatic, since most of the terrestrial species may be found in aquatic habitats. *Propappus* is an aquatic genus, but as yet we have no species recorded. *Cernosvitoviella atrata* (Bretscher) can be regarded as aquatic, and many species of *Analycus* (= *Mesenchytraeus*) are found in wet soils. *Marionina riparia* Bretscher is a species commonly found in fresh-water, but it too is not recorded from Britain as yet. Several species of *Henlea* and *Buchholzia* may also be encountered.

Full descriptions of many species can be found in Nielsen & Christensen (1959), and keys in Ude (1929). Revisions of the genera diagnoses are in Brinkhurst & Jamieson (1971). Note the substitution of *Distichopus* Leidy for *Fridericia*, and the resurrection of *Grania* (see also Lasserre 1967).

Family LUMBRICULIDAE and Family DORYDRILIDAE

These two families have been reviewed in their entirety by D. G. Cook (see Cook in Brinkhurst & Jamieson, 1971) and the British species were described by him (Cook 1967); this account is derived from his work.

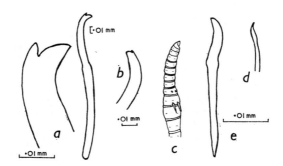

Fig. 13.   *a*, chaetae of *Lumbriculus variegatus*;
           b, chaeta and *c*, penes of *Stylodrilus heringianus*;
           d, dorsal and *e*, ventral chaetae of *Haplotaxis gordioides*.

The genus *Dorydrilus* was included in the family Lumbriculidae until recently (it was placed there by Cook 1967), but it has now been recognized as constituting an interesting small family together with the very poorly known genus *Lycodrilus,* which is endemic to Lake Baikal. Whilst the chaetal arrangement is like that of *Trichodrilus,* the reproductive organs of *Dorydrilus* are of the same plan as those in the Tubificidae, Naididae and other families of the sub-order Tubificina of the order Haplotaxida, as opposed to those of the other two orders of Oligochaeta (Moniligastrida, Lumbriculida) which comprise the single families the Moniligastridae and Lumbriculidae (Brinkhurst & Jamieson, 1971).

The two families are dealt with here because of the external similarities which may lead many to classify *Dorydrilus* specimens as lumbriculids in their collections.

1   Chaetae all or mostly bifid (fig. 13)—   2

—   Chaetae all single pointed—   3

2   Anterior segments bearing distinct secondary annuli. Posterior lateral blood vessels indistinct, unbranched (fig. 14*f*). Mature specimens with long, non-retractile penes on X (figs. 13*c*, 15*b*)—
Stylodrilus heringianus Clap.

The worms are unpigmented except for the blood system and the chloragogen cells around the gut, most specimens being white to reddish in colour. The worm looks like a tubificid and coils in the same way as most members of that family. It is known from lakes and streams all over Britain, commonly in sandy, unproductive habitats. It appears to be intolerant of organic pollution.

—   Anterior segments not bearing secondary annuli. Posterior lateral blood vessels well developed and branched (fig. 14*a*). Sexual specimens rare, but without non-retractile penes—
Lumbriculus variegatus (Müller)

The living worm is red-brown in colour with a slight green colouration superimposed anteriorly. It swims with spiral undulations, and is common in all sorts of habitats. It can form resistant cysts, thin cuticular structures to which adhere particles of the substratum. Earlier speculations regarding the identity of cyst-forming oligochaetes as *Lamprodrilus mrazeki* are hence disposed of, and that species must be removed from the British list.

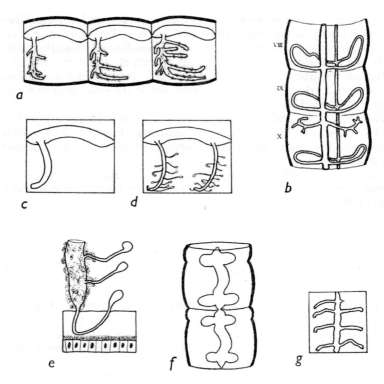

Fig. 14.   Lumbriculidae: vascular system.
Lumbriculus variegatus:
    a, range of variation in posterior lateral blood vessels (lateral view).
    b, part of anterior vascular system (dorsal view).
Eclipidrilus lacustris:
    c, lateral blood vessels of xvi-xxiii.
    d, lateral blood vessels of xxiv on
    e, posterior lateral blood vessel showing blind caeca entering longitudinal muscle layer.
Stylodrilus heringianus:
    f, dorsal blood vessel in posterior segments showing small lateral pouches.
Trichodrilus cantabrigiensis:
    g, posterior lateral blood vessels.
(from *J. Zool.* **153,** pp. 353-368).

3 (1) Chaetae robust. Single median spermatheca in IX, single median atrium in X (figs. 14a, b, 15a)—
Eclipidrilus lacustris (Verrill)
(*Stylodrilus* sp. nov. of the first edition of this key)

Llyn Tegid, Merioneth; Blakemere, Shropshire; otherwise St. Lawrence Great Lakes of North America.
The distribution of this species seems unusual at least, but *Sparganophilus tamesis* (= *eiseni*) has a similar distribution if a little wider in Europe. The introduction of the North American tubificid *Limnodrilus cervix* is well established (Kennedy 1965). The possibility of introduction through Liverpool or the earlier port at Parkgate (Wirral) should be considered. The worm may swim energetically with lateral undulations.

— Chaetae thin, needle-like. Spermathecae paired in X or two pairs, in XI and XII; atria paired in X—   4

4 Posterior lateral blood vessels absent from the dorsal vessel— 5

— Posterior lateral blood vessels present on dorsal vessel (fig. 14g)—   6

5 Two pairs of spermathecae, in XI and XII. Atria and penes relatively small (fig. 15d)—   **Trichodrilus hrabei** Cook

Small gravel-bottomed stream at Llangadwaladr, Denbighshire. Possibly also Sidlow Bridge, River Mole, Surrey and College Pond, Bangor, Caerns; immature specimens only — Brinkhurst collection.

— One pair of spermathecae in X. Atria and penes relatively large (fig. 15e)—   **Dorydrilus michaelseni** Piguet

Stream at Llangadwaladr, Denbighshire, only one specimen.

6 (4) Posterior pair of vasa deferentia do not penetrate septum 10/11. Pharyngeal glands extend to VIII—
Trichodrilus cantabrigiensis (Beddard)

Waterbeach, Cambridgeshire. The species is known only from Beddard's types in the B.M. (Nat. Hist.). The species differs little from the European *T. allobrogum* Clap.

48 LUMBRICULIDAE, DORYDRILIDAE

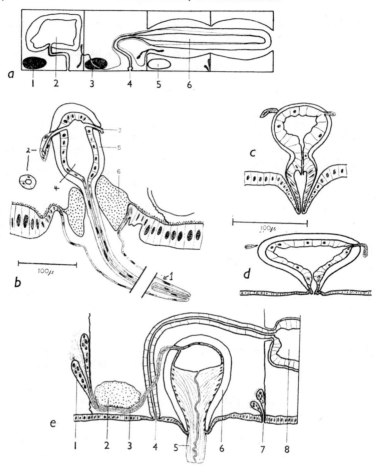

Fig. 15. Dorydrilidae and Lumbriculidae: reproductive system.

    a, Eclipidrilus lacustris, male and female reproductive system, lateral view.

      (1-anterior testes, 2-spermathecal ampulla, 3-posterior testes, 4-male pore (median on X), 5-ovary, 6-atrium).

    b, Stylodrilus heringianus, atrium and penis of one side, in L.S.

      (1-penis, 2-anterior vas deferens, 3-posterior vas deferens, 4-atrial lumen, 5-atrial muscle, 6-circular muscle).

    c, Trichodrilus cantabrigiensis, atrium and penis of one side, L.S.

    d, Trichodrilus hrabei, atrium and penis of one side, L.S.

    e, Dorydrilus michaelseni, reproductive organs, one side in L.S.

      (1-male funnel, 2-ovary, 3-vas deferens, 4-spermathecal pore, 5-penis, partly protruded, 6-atrial muscles, 7-female pore, 8-spermathecal ampulla).

(from *J. Zool.* **153,** pp. 353–368).

— Posterior pair of vasa deferentia penetrate septum 10/11. Pharyngeal glands extend to VII—
Trichodrilus icenorum Beddard

Trichodrilus lengersdorfi Michaelsen
In a well (now apparently filled in) at Pulham St. Mary, Norfolk.
This species, like *T. cantabrigiensis*, is known only from the type specimens. The specific distinction between it and *T. icenorum* depends on few characters. When a large collection becomes available for study, these may prove to vary intraspecifically.

Rhynchelmis limosella Hoffmeister
This species was reported by Percival and Whitehead from the River Wharfe, Yorkshire, but the record was not confirmed by any recognized authority. An immature specimen in the B.M. (Nat. Hist.) described by Friend from a water supply at Ringwood, Hants is clearly referrable to the genus but not to any particular species.

Stylodrilus brachystylus Hrabe
Specimens from a stream in Heddons Valley, Hunters Inn, Devon were placed in the B.M. (Nat. Hist.) collection by Cernosvitov. The validity of the identification is in doubt as the material was not fully mature.

While one or two more species of genera, such as *Stylodrilus* and *Trichodrilus,* may be added to the British list in time, these will certainly be restricted to a few localities. Most biologists will encounter only *Stylodrilus heringianus* and *Lumbriculus variegatus* in their normal work; groundwater situations may yield a more respectable list of species.

Family GLOSSOSCOLECIDAE

Of all the families of 'megadrile' or earthworm-like worms forming the sub-order Lumbricina of the order Haplotaxida, this family contains the majority of truly aquatic genera and species (Brinkhurst & Jamieson, in press). Only one species is recorded from Britain.

Sparganophilus tamesis Benham

60–200 mm × 1·5–5 mm, 125–260 segs.   Body cylindrical, preserved specimens frequently with a deep dorsal groove. Anus dorso-terminal.   Chaetae ornamented distally with one to few irregular jagged ridges.   Clitellum from 14–16 to 24–27. Prostate-like glands on one or more of III to X and (XVI) XXIII to XXV, XXVI or XXVII.   Male pores inconspicuous in XIX.   Female pores XIV.   Spermathecal pores inconspicuous in VI/VII to VIII/IX.

(*Pelodrilus cuenoti* Tetry, *S. eiseni* Smith, ?*S. elongatus* (Friend))

> Recorded from the Thames (Goring, ?Oxford); ?R. Cherwell, Oxford; ?lily tank in Cornwall; (Lake) Windermere; Cheshire Meres, also from France and North America.   Found amongst the roots of water plants.

Family BRANCHIOBDELLIDAE

This is a family of small worms 3–12 mm long, the western European species belonging to the one genus *Branchiobdella*.   *B. parasita* Henle inhabits the gills, thorax or the tail of crayfish, chiefly *Astacus astacus*.   It has no chaetae but bears strongly toothed jaws.

Ude (1929) gives a key to the four species commonly found in Germany.   A more complete account is to be found in Georgévitch (1956).

Branchiobdella astari Odier has been recorded from Reading by Leeke & Price (1965).

Family HAPLOTAXIDAE

Only one European freshwater species, *Haplotaxis gordioides* (Hartmann) is known from Britain.   This is immediately recognisable from its great length (up to 300 mm) and its thread-like form. The chaetae are also characteristic, the dorsal ones being much smaller than the ventral, and absent in posterior segments (fig. 13*d*, *e*).   There is a single chaeta in each bundle.

Family LUMBRICIDAE

Principally terrestrial in habit (see Gerard 1963 for a full account). I have commonly encountered *Eiseniella tetraedra* (Savigny) in aquatic habitats. In var. *macrura* the male pores are on segment XIII and the clitellum on segments XV to XXII, whereas in var. *hercynia* the male pores are on segment XV and the clitellum on segments XXII or XXIII to XXVI or XXVII.

ACKNOWLEDGEMENTS

It is with great pleasure that I acknowledge the assistance rendered to me in the preparation of this manuscript by Mr H. C. Gilson and Drs T. T. Macan, T. B. Reynoldson, R. W. Simms, C. O. Nielsen and H. B. N. Hynes. Dr C. Sperber was kind enough to allow me to reproduce her figures of naidid chaetae. I must also record my gratitude to Miss J. Findlay, who prepared most of the material for microscopical examination, and thus enabled me to see more specimens than would otherwise have been possible. For the provision of a grant which financed this technical assistance I am indebted to the Nature Conservancy.

The revised version relies heavily on contributions by Dr D. G. Cook.

REFERENCES

Brinkhurst, R. O. (1960). Introductory studies on the British Tubificidae (Oligochaeta). *Arch. Hydrobiol.* **56,** 395–412.

Brinkhurst, R. O. (1962-3). A check list of British Oligochaeta. *Proc. zool. Soc. Lond.* **138,** 317–330; **140,** 315.

Brinkhurst, R. O. (1963a). Taxonomical studies on the Tubificidae (Annelida; Oligochaeta). *Int. Revue ges. Hydrobiol. Hydrogr. Syst. Beih.* **2,** 1–89.

Brinkhurst, R. O. (1963b). A genus of brackish-water Oligochaeta new to Britain. *Nature, Lond.* **199,** 1206.

Brinkhurst, R. O. (1963c). Notes on the brackish-water and marine species of Tubificidae (Annelida, Oligochaeta). *J. mar. biol. Ass. U.K.* **43,** 709–715.

Brinkhurst, R. O. (1964a). The biology of the Tubificidae. *Verh. int. Verein. theor. angew. Limnol.* **15,** 855–863.

Brinkhurst, R. O. (1964b). Observations on the biology of lake-dwelling Tubificidae. *Arch. Hydrobiol.* **60,** 385–418.

Brinkhurst, R. O. (1964c). Observations on the biology of the marine oligochaete worm *Tubifex costatus* (Claparède). *J. mar. biol. Ass. U.K.* **44,** 11–16.

Brinkhurst, R. O. (1965). The biology of the Tubificidae with special reference to pollution. *Biological problems in water pollution,* 3rd Seminar, 1962, 57–65.

Brinkhurst, R. O. (1966). Oligochaeta in *Limnofauna Europea,* 110–117.

Brinkhurst, R. O. & Jamieson, B. G. M. (1971). *The Aquatic Oligochaeta of the World.* Edinburgh: Oliver & Boyd (in press).

Burke, D. (1967). Zur Morphologie und Systematik der Aeolosomatidæ Beddard, 1895 und Potamodrilidæ nov. fam. (Oligochæta). *Zool. Jb. (Syst.)* 94, 187-368.

Černosvitov, L. (1942). A revision of Friend's types and descriptions of British Oligochaeta. *Proc. zool. Soc. Lond.* B, 111, 237–280.

Georgévitch, J. (1956). Branchiobdellides de Yugoslavie. *Bull. Acad. serbe Sci.* 222, 6d. *Cl. Sci. math. nat.* 10, No. 8, 47–76.

Gerard, B. M. (1963). Synopses of the British fauna. No. 6 Lumbricidae (Annelida), 2nd ed. London: Linnean Society.

Kennedy, C. R. (1965). The distribution and habitat of *Limnodrilus* Claparède. *Oikos* 16, 26–38.

Lasserre, P. (1967). Oligochètes marins des côtes de France. *Cah. Biol. mar.* 8, 273–293.

Leeke, C. J. & Price, A. (1965). *Branchiobdella astaci* Odier (Oligochaeta, Annelida) in Reading. *Reading Nat.* No. 17, 18–19.

Nielsen, C. O. & Christensen, B. (1959). The Enchytraeidae . . . . *Natura jutl.,* 8-9, 1–160.

Southern, R. (1909). Contributions towards a monograph of the British and Irish Oligochaeta. *Proc. R. Ir. Acad.* (B) 27, 119–182.

Sperber, C. (1948). A taxonomic study of the Naididae. *Zool. Bidr., Upps.,* 28, 1–296.

Sperber, C. (1950). A guide for the determination of European Naididae. *Zool. Bidr., Upps.,* 29, 45–78.

Stephenson, J. (1930). The Oligochaeta. Oxford: Clarendon Press.

Ude, H. (1929). Oligochaeta. *Tierwelt Dtl.,* 15, 1–132.

INDEX

Names in parentheses are synonyms. Species in square brackets have not been recorded in Britain. Bold figures indicate illustrations.